THE
STAFFORDSHIRE
HOARD

Birmingham Museums

Copyright © Birmingham
Museums Trust, 2014

First published in Great Britain in 2014
by Birmingham Museums Trust,
Chamberlain Square,
Birmingham, B3 3DH
www.birminghammuseums.org.uk

ISBN 978-0-9570494-4-4

A catalogue record is available from
the British Library.

Author: Dr David Symons

Designed by Sacha Davison Lunt

Printed in the UK by EPC Direct Ltd.

All photographs are ©Birmingham
Museums Trust unless credited
otherwise below:
p.15 (illustration): Trevor Bounford
p. 8-9: Portable Antiquities Scheme
p. 62 right: Liverpool Museums

CONTENTS

DIRECTOR'S FOREWORD

The Staffordshire Hoard is that rare thing, an archaeological find that has captured the imaginations of academics and the public. It is a discovery of international significance that is transforming our understanding of Anglo-Saxon England. The hoard was deposited at a time of great social, political and religious turbulence, and the extraordinary wealth, variety, imagery and technological expertise of the objects reflect this.

It is frustrating that we do not know who owned the hoard, or why it came to be buried in a field in Staffordshire. Perhaps it is King Penda's war chest, or an offering to the gods, or loot from a battlefield. But this very uncertainty is part of the Hoard's fascination, because everyone can have a theory, and anyone might be right.

Birmingham City Council and Stoke-on-Trent Council are joint owners of the hoard, and it forms part of the collections of Birmingham Museums and Stoke-on-Trent Museums. The owners are grateful to a horde of funders for their contributions to the acquisition, research and conservation of the hoard to date. The new displays in Birmingham Museum and Art Gallery present a selection of items from the hoard in a way that explains how they were made, used and destroyed, reflecting the results of the research programme. I should like to thank the Heritage Lottery Fund, Garfield Weston, the City of Birmingham Museums and Art Gallery Development Trust, the Friends of Birmingham Museums Trust, Arts Council England, and the J Paul Getty Jnr Charitable Trust for their generous support for this project.

Ellen McAdam

DISCOVERY

The Staffordshire Hoard is the
largest collection of Anglo-Saxon
gold and silver ever discovered.
It was found in a field near the
village of Hammerwich, in south
Staffordshire. Other Anglo-Saxon
sites have produced remarkable
finds, but none come close to the
scale of the Staffordshire Hoard.
It contains over 4,000 objects and
fragments and includes over 5 kg
(about 11 lbs) of gold and almost
1½ kg (3.3 lbs) of silver.

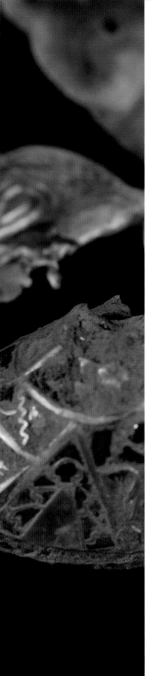

DISCOVERY, EXCAVATION, ACQUISITION

The first pieces of the hoard were discovered on 5 July 2009 by local metal-detector user Terry Herbert, who reported his discovery to Duncan Slarke, Finds Liaison Officer for the Portable Antiquities Scheme for Staffordshire and the West Midlands. Realising how important the find was, Slarke contacted the Staffordshire County Council archaeology team who visited the site to assess whether there might be any more objects to be recovered. They found pieces of gold literally lying on the surface of the field.

Birmingham Archaeology, a field research company based at the University of Birmingham, was commissioned to excavate the site to see if there was any other archaeological evidence, and to recover the rest of the hoard. The excavation lasted four weeks and covered an area of 155 sq.m.

The site is located close to the Anglo-Saxon centres of Lichfield and Tamworth, on the edge of a hill overlooking Watling Street, an old Roman road which was still an important route in the seventh century (today it is the A5). Remarkably, all the objects were found in the plough soil, within a few inches of the surface.

The hoard is thought to have been deeper underground originally, with years of soil erosion gradually bringing the objects closer to the surface. When the field was ploughed in autumn 2008, the hoard was disturbed and spread through the soil. The excavators found no Anglo-Saxon features where the hoard had been buried: there were no buildings, no burials, and no signs of a battle. All the evidence suggests that the hoard was hidden in a wild area, far from any human settlement.

On 24 September 2009, the hoard was declared Treasure at a coroner's inquest. With the help of record donations from the public and some major grants, the cities of Birmingham and Stoke-on-Trent jointly acquired the hoard in March 2010. In May 2013 a private donation allowed for the acquisition of 81 additional pieces of the hoard discovered following a second survey of the field in November 2012.

THE HOARD

The vast majority of the identified objects in the hoard were for use in war, mainly parts of swords and helmets, but there are also Christian crosses, and a biblical inscription. Almost all the items are made of gold and silver, and have mostly been stripped from other objects.

The most elaborate kind of Anglo-Saxon sword had a metal pommel cap at the top of the handle as well as metal guard plates and other fittings. We know that 85 swords of this kind are represented in the hoard, but the total number could be much higher. The hoard also contains a large number of mounts that may have come from simpler sword handles, which did not have a metal pommel cap and guard plates, but instead were decorated with small filigree and cloisonné mounts. Both kinds of sword would have belonged to the top ranks of Anglo-Saxon society.

The Anglo-Saxons regarded swords as prestige items. Most Anglo-Saxon men were farmers or craftsmen and would have gone into battle with just a wooden shield, a spear and a knife. Only the most important men had a sword, mail armour and a helmet, and only the nobility and the elite warriors of the king's household would have used swords with gold and silver handles.

The lack of any other archaeological evidence and the diversity of the items have made dating the hoard difficult. Based on the style of decoration and the typology of the objects found, we think the hoard was hidden around 650-670.

Unfortunately, we do not know who buried it, or why they did so. Archaeologists have suggested a range of possibilities – the hoard was loot from a battle, a ransom for a king, or a royal treasure chest; it was hidden to protect it from raiders, it was plunder hidden by raiders who were being chased, it was an offering to the gods, to name just a few. Further research may shed more light on this problem, but it is likely that we will never know what really happened.

Gold mounts from the Staffordshire Hoard. OPPOSITE TOP *K464, l: 47 mm;* OPPOSITE LEFT *K1465, l: 18 mm;* OPPOSITE RIGHT *K16, l: 24.4 mm*

THE ANGLO-SAXONS

Around 410 the Romans lost control of Britain and local British rulers seized power, with some of them hiring mercenaries from Germany as protection against Scottish and Irish raiders. In 441-2 these mercenaries reportedly rebelled against their employers, invited other settlers from Germany, and soon controlled much of eastern England.

The historian Bede, our main source for the history of the period, wrote in 731 that many different peoples settled in England in the fifth century, including Angles, Saxons, Jutes, Frisians, Danes, and Huns. Over the next 400 years they gradually pushed west, forcing many of the British back into Wales and Cornwall. However, modern DNA studies suggest that many other Britons did not flee west, but stayed put and integrated into the new society. Eventually the descendants of all these peoples came to think of themselves as 'English', with a common cultural identity and sharing the same language, Old English, an early form of English.

Over the years, these new settlers took over existing communities and established new ones. Groups in the West Midlands included the Tomsæte, 'dwellers of the Tame valley', who lived around Tamworth, and the Beormingas, 'people of Beorma', who gave their name to Birmingham. Gradually these small groups came together to form larger units. In the seventh century, bigger kingdoms were created as successful kings conquered their neighbours. By 700, seven kingdoms had emerged – Northumbria, Mercia, East Anglia, Essex, Kent, Sussex and Wessex. By 825 only Northumbria, Mercia, East Anglia and Wessex survived.

Mercia

Kingdoms under
Mercian domination

N

0
|————————| 100 kms
0
|————————| 100 miles

NORTHUMBRIA

North Sea

Irish Sea

POWYS

MERCIA

EAST
ANGLIA

ESSEX

WESSEX

KENT

SUSSEX

English Channel

The map shows the
situation when Mercia
was at its height, in c.790.

MERCIA, AN ANGLO-BRITISH KINGDOM

At the time of burial, in the middle of seventh century, the area where the hoard was discovered was at the heart of the kingdom of Mercia. 'Mercia', from the Old English *Mierce* means 'the Marches', the borderlands between the English and the Welsh. It was created by native Britons and incoming Saxons in the seventh century and destroyed by the Vikings in the 870s. Mercia was often at war with the other Anglo-Saxon kingdoms. Its most warlike king, Penda (reigned around 626-655), fought many battles, especially against East Anglia and Northumbria. His successors made Mercia the most powerful kingdom in England in the eighth century, stretching from Wales to East Anglia and from the Humber to the Thames.

675-704
Aethelred, Penda's son, is king of Mercia.

725-825
Mercia dominates the other English kingdoms.

731
Bede completes his *History of the English Church and People*, our main source for the history of Britain from the late sixth to the early eighth century.

757-96
Offa is king of Mercia. Offa's Dyke is built, an earthwork marking the border between Mercia and Wales.

793
Viking raiders attack Lindisfarne; many more attacks follow in the coming years.

825-9
Wessex becomes the dominant Anglo-Saxon kingdom.

865
The Viking 'Great Army' arrives in England. In the next ten years it conquers East Anglia, Northumbria, and Mercia. It is finally defeated by King Alfred of Wessex in 878.

927
Aethelstan, Alfred's grandson, becomes the first king of all England.

978-1016
Aethelred II is king of England. New Viking attacks begin.

1016-42
Vikings conquer England and three Danish kings, Cnut, Harold I and Harthacnut, rule the country in succession

1042
Edward the Confessor, Aethelred II's son, becomes king of England.

1066
The battle of Hastings leads to the Norman Conquest of England.

TIMELINE

The Anglo-Saxon period lasted from around 450 to 1066 AD. It was the time when the idea of England and the English people was formed.

410

Conventional date for the end of Roman Britain.

AROUND 450

Anglo-Saxon settlement begins in Britain.

AROUND 500

The Anglo-Saxons are heavily defeated by the British at Mount Badon.

AROUND 550

Gildas, a British monk, writes *The Ruin of Britain*, the only contemporary account of this period.

597

St Augustine is sent from Rome and begins his mission for the conversion of the Anglo-Saxons.

AROUND 625

The Sutton Hoo ship burial, possibly the burial of a king of East Anglia.

632

Kings Penda of Mercia and Cadwallon of Gwynedd defeat and kill King Edwin of Northumbria.

642

King Penda's Mercians defeat and kill King Oswald of Northumbria.

655

King Penda is defeated and killed at Winwaed (near Doncaster).

658-75

Wulfhere, Penda's son, is king of Mercia.

669

St Chad is made the first bishop of Lichfield and establishes the first cathedral there.

650-670

THE STAFFORDSHIRE HOARD IS BURIED

THE TREASURY

Handle for a seax, or single-edged knife, made up of five pieces that contain over 80 gr (about three ounces) of gold. This is one of the most spectacular objects in the hoard with especially fine cloisonné garnet decoration. The pieces that sat at the top and bottom of the handgrip have animal interlace decoration. 'Seax' describes any kind of single-edged knife, from a short knife used for whittling wood and eating, to a large war knife that was essentially a short sword. The name 'Saxons' probably means 'people of the knife'.

LEFT TO RIGHT *K449, w: 31 mm; K370, w: 29.6 mm; K690, w: 33.3 mm; K354, w: 32.4 mm; K376, w: 28.9 mm*

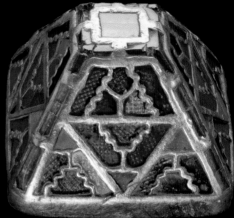

Pair of gold sword pyramids, with cloisonné garnet and blue glass decoration. We think that these pyramids were fastened to the ends of a leather band, which was attached to the sword's scabbard – and could be tied around the handle of the sword. This stopped the sword accidentally falling out of the scabbard, but it also reduced the chance of the sword being drawn in anger, since the owner had to untie the band first. Bands like these are called 'peace bands' in the slightly later Viking sagas.

LEFT *K377, w: 21.2 mm;* RIGHT *K462, w: 22.4 mm*

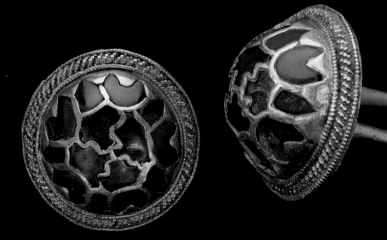

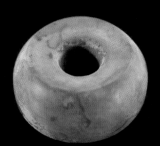

Pair of gold sword 'buttons', with cloisonné garnet decoration, and a stone bead. Both these 'buttons' may originally have been set in stone beads, but only one bead was found in the hoard. They may have been used like the sword pyramids, fastened to the ends of a leather thong that tied the sword into its scabbard. A pair of very similar 'buttons' was found on top of the sword scabbard in the Sutton Hoo ship burial.

TOP LEFT *K1425, h: 15.09 mm;* RIGHT *K675, h: 16.44 mm;* BOTTOM *K764, h: 10.05 mm*

OPPOSITE
Christened 'The Mystery Object'
by the hoard research team, this is
decorated with very fine cloisonné
garnet work, small gold panels
with pairs of biting beasts and, at
the top, a glass 'gem' which is the
largest piece of glass in the hoard.
Nothing like it has ever been found
before and no one has been able to
suggest a convincing identification
for it yet. Among the suggestions
made so far are that it is part of
the boss from the centre of a
shield, the lid to a Christian
chalice, the stopper to a drinking
horn, or part of the headgear of
a high-ranking priest.

TOP TO BOTTOM *K545, K1055, K130, overall
h: c.70 mm;*

ABOVE
Gold pommel cap, decorated with
large, highly polished cloisonné
garnets of deep red colour. The
garnets along the upper edge have
been cut with a curved, instead
of a flat, face, which would have
been difficult to do.

K1160, l: 40.5 mm

Silver gilt pommel cap, with decoration combining filigree and cabochon garnets. 'Cabochon' describes a gemstone which has been cut with a convex top which projects above its mount. This is one of just a few objects in the hoard that combines filigree and garnet decoration.

K294, l: 52 mm

Pair of gold hilt collars, decorated with filigree and cabochon garnets. They come from the handle of a sword or a knife. The larger one (K454) would have been set at the bottom of the handgrip and the smaller one (K1000) at the top. It is possible to read the decoration as a human face, with the garnets as the eyes, or as two birds, with the garnets serving as their heads.

LEFT *K1000, l: 25 mm;* RIGHT *K454, l: c.35 mm*

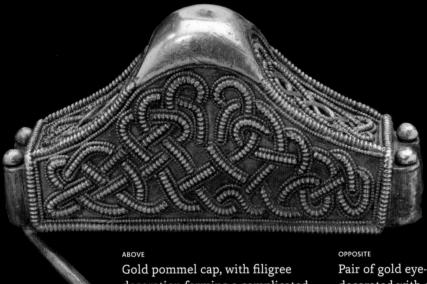

ABOVE

Gold pommel cap, with filigree decoration forming a complicated interlace pattern, skilfully executed by the metalworker.

K1200, l: 39.8 mm

OPPOSITE

Pair of gold eye-shaped mounts, decorated with cloisonné garnets. Each has an outer band of spectacular cloisonné garnet decoration and an inner band which originally contained another filling, but we are not sure what this was. The central setting of each mount has a reflective gold foil. This suggests that it probably contained something like a garnet or a piece of coloured glass that would have allowed light to pass through and be reflected back from the gold.

TOP K270, l: c.75 mm; BOTTOM K843, l: 72 mm

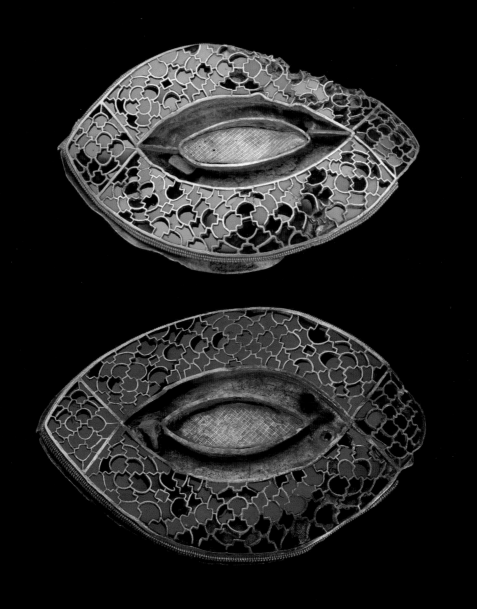

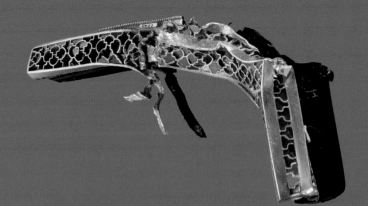

Gold edging strips, decorated with cloisonné garnets. They may be mounts from the cover of a book, probably a Bible or gospel book. They all have the same decoration on three sides and a recess on the fourth side. The book cover would have slotted into the recesses.

BOTTOM *K356, l: 80.8 mm;* CENTRE *K357, l: 46.6 mm;* TOP RIGHT *K665, l (distorted): 53 mm;* TOP LEFT *K1145, l: 40.9 mm*

OPPOSITE

Pair of gold mounts, decorated with very fine cloisonné garnets. Their shape is unusual and hard to interpret. Traces of bone inlay can be seen on K653.

TOP *K653, l: 56 mm;* BOTTOM *K654, l: 58.4 mm*

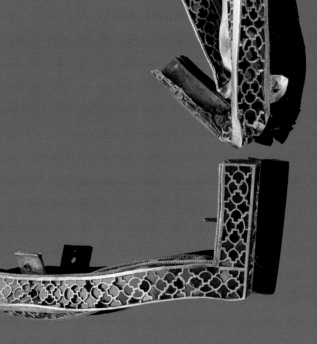

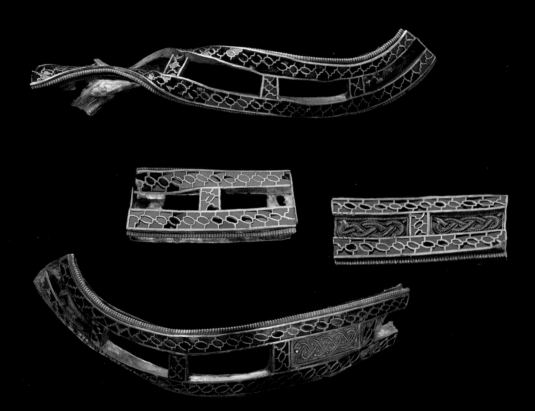

Gold slotted strips, decorated with cloisonné garnets and small filigree panels. These strips all have the same cloisonné decoration and also have rectangular slots in them. Some of these slots still contain panels with interlaced animal designs in filigree, but most are empty. The hoard contained many loose panels which may eventually be fitted back into the empty slots. These strips may possibly have decorated a saddle.

TOP *K371, l: 105 mm;*
CENTRE LEFT *K696, l: 40 mm;*
CENTRE RIGHT *K677, l: 41.7 mm;*
BOTTOM *K275, l: 96.1 mm;*

FRONT AND BACK VIEW

Gold inscribed strip. The purpose of this strip is still not certain, but it may be one arm of a cross that was attached to a container for a sacred relic. A version of the same text is engraved on each side.

On one side the letters have been filled with niello, a black material made from a mixture of metallic sulphides, which makes them stand out black against the gold.

The inscription is in Latin (with two spelling mistakes!) and comes from the Bible (Numbers, 10:35). It reads *'Surge domine et disepentur [dissipentur] inimici tui et fugent [fugiant] qui oderunt te a facie tua'*, which translates as *"Arise, O Lord, and may your enemies be scattered and may those who hate you flee from your face"*.

K550, l: 89.5 mm

OPPOSITE

The Folded Cross, made of gold and set with cabochon garnets. One of the garnets had been broken and carefully repaired with a small strip of gold in the seventh century. The cross was intentionally dismantled, before it was added in the hoard. The mounts fixed to it were prised off and all but two of the garnets set in them were removed. The cross was then folded up and the loose mounts were tucked inside it. The cross may originally have been mounted on the front cover of a leather-bound Bible.

K655, l: 21.3 mm

LEFT

Gold pectoral cross. The arms are decorated with filigree and there is a large garnet in the centre. This cross would originally have hung around the neck of a high-ranking churchman, noble or even a king or queen. The shape is very similar to that of the cross buried with St Cuthbert when he died in 687.

K303, w: 66.1 mm

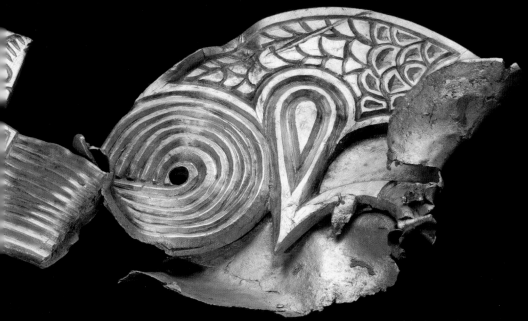

Gold plaque in the shape of two
birds of prey clutching a fish
between them. It may have been
fastened to the front of a shield
or been used to decorate a
saddle. The plaque was badly
damaged when removed from
the original object.

K652, l: c.120 mm

Gold mount in the shape of a horse's head, with very fine filigree decoration. When it was first discovered, the animal was identified as either a horse or a seahorse. Closer examination has suggested that there was originally a horse's head at each end of the mount.

K1497, l: 420 mm

Gold hilt plate from a seax or single-edged knife. Most seaxes had quite plain handles, but this hilt plate must have belonged to a magnificent knife. It is decorated with two lines of interlinked animals, each biting the leg of the animal in front. There are four animals to each side of the central blade hole. Both groups are facing in the same direction, with their heads pointed towards the cutting edge of the blade. Very similar animals appear in the *Book of Durrow*, an illuminated manuscript made around 650-700.

K567, l: 73.5 mm

Silver gilt object with bands of animal decoration. The animals in two of the bands reach back to bite their own bodies. Many people think this is a cheek piece from a helmet, while others disagree and think it is too small to be a cheek piece.

K453, l: 100 mm

U-shaped gold strip and gold horse head. The horse head fits into one end of the strip, which has animal decoration along each side. They may belong to a crest from the top of a helmet.

TOP *K546, l: c.180 mm*; BOTTOM *K678, l: 47.8 mm*

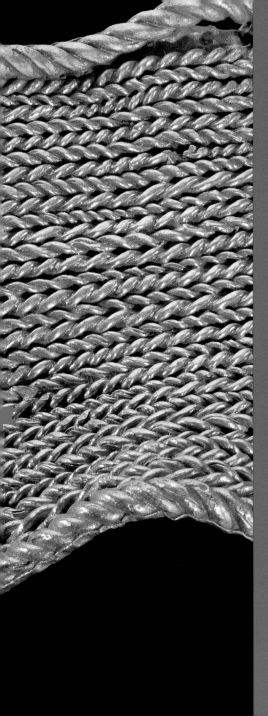

CRAFT TECHNIQUES

THE METALWORKERS

Many objects in the Staffordshire Hoard are of the highest workmanship. The seventh-century metalworkers who produced them were astonishingly skilled and would have been greatly valued. Later Anglo-Saxon evidence suggests that they lived in the households of kings, important nobles or leading churchmen and made whatever these men required. However, no matter how talented they were, the metalworkers did not have the same status as the warriors whose weapons they made and decorated.

Most of the objects in the hoard were made in England. Some are typical of material that has been found in East Anglia and Kent, while others may have been made in Mercia or Northumbria.

We think that Anglo-Saxon bronzesmiths and goldsmiths largely used the same basic tools. A set of bronzesmith's tools found in a grave at Tattershall Thorpe in Lincolnshire in 1981, included a hammer, tongs, snips, drawbar and anvil, together with a scale pan and weights, and a box of scrap metal. The smiths would have melted the metal in a crucible over a hearth, using bellows to raise the temperature of the fire. When it had melted, the metal was poured into moulds of various shapes and reworked as required.

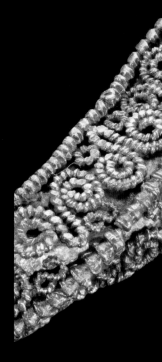

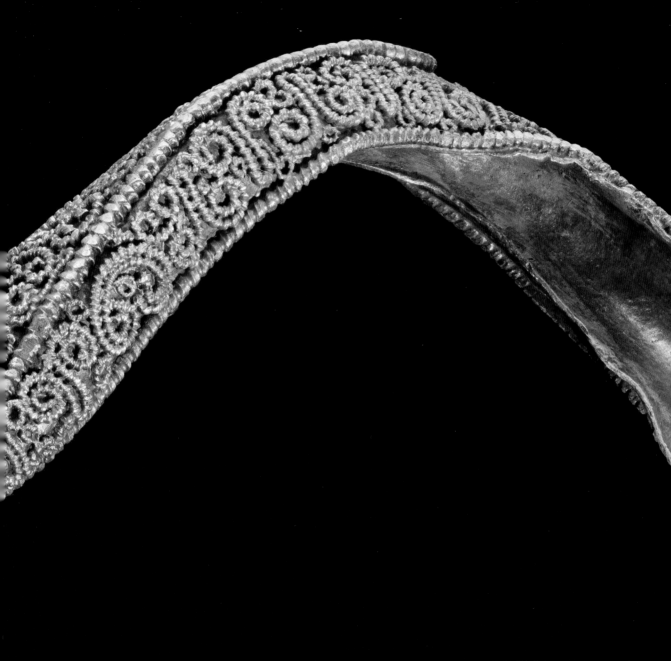

Gold hilt collar with filigree decoration.
K699, l: 53.0 mm

RAW MATERIALS

GOLD

Although small amounts of gold occurred naturally in the British Isles, the gold used in the hoard probably came from recycling old, broken or unwanted objects, or from Byzantine coins that had reached Western Europe in trade or as tribute payments and been melted down.

SILVER

The Anglo-Saxon historian Bede, writing in 731, lists silver among the metals found in England. He does not say where it was mined, but we know that the Romans extracted silver from lead ores found in the Mendip Hills in Somerset and the Derbyshire Peak District, and the Anglo-Saxons probably did the same. Old silver coins and other objects would also have been recycled.

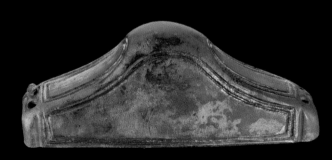

Silver pommel cap.
K456, l: 50 mm

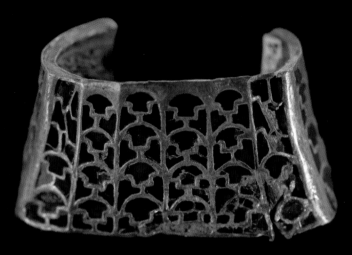

Fragments of a gold
hilt collar decorated
with cloisonné garnets.
K104, l: 32.9 mm

GARNETS

Garnets (red-coloured, semi-
precious stones) are found in
many places around the world,
but scientific analysis carried out
in 2010 at the C2RMF, a research
laboratory at the Louvre Museum
in Paris, suggested that the garnets
used in the hoard may have come
from northern India and the Czech
Republic. These garnets would have
passed from merchant to merchant
until they finally reached England,
probably as unworked stones which
were cut to size and shape by the
Anglo-Saxon craftsmen.

GLASS

Analysis carried out at the British
Museum suggests that the white
and blue glass used in the hoard is
probably made from reused Roman
glass. The composition of the red
glass is slightly different. This
might also be reused glass,
or it could have been imported
from the Rhineland, where a lot
of glass was still being made in
the seventh century.

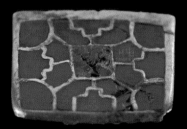

Rectangular gold
mount, decorated with
cloisonné garnets
and a central panel
of blue glass, which
is probably reused
Roman glass.
K1226, l: 15.3 mm

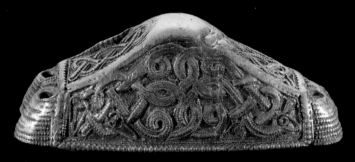

Gold pommel cap, decorated with filigree showing four serpents. Although the pattern is quite stylised, the interlaced animals can still be identified. *K457, l: 42.3 mm*

Gold mount in the shape of an eagle decorated with cloisonné garnets. Eagles feature prominently in Germanic art and myth and they are often used to decorate objects connected with feasting and war. *K1084, l: 22.3 mm*

ABOVE
Two gold snakes, each with eyes and a tongue that sticks out. Three pairs of snakes were found in the hoard. They were originally fixed to larger objects, but we do not know what these were.

Snakes were sacred to the god Woden and were connected with healing, fertility and the underworld. LEFT *K816, l: 37.0 mm,* RIGHT *K1014, l: 50 mm*

DESIGNS

GERMANIC INFLUENCES

The Anglo-Saxons were part of a wider Germanic world that extended across northern Germany, Scandinavia, the Low Countries and England. Connected by the North Sea, they shared a pagan, warrior culture, and were linked by similar beliefs and gods. People, objects and influences travelled freely across the area. Most of the objects in the hoard are decorated in a common Germanic style based on the interlaced bodies of stylised animals. On the earliest pieces in the hoard the animals' bodies are stretched out into long, thin ribbons which are interlaced to form symmetrical patterns. With time, the animals become more and more abstract. They lose their legs and eventually become impossible to recognise as animals. Other items from the hoard are decorated with boars, snakes and birds of prey that were also common Germanic motifs. Although most were made in England, a few pieces in the hoard were made in Germany or Scandinavia.

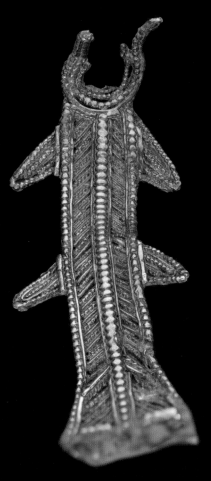

Silver pommel cap, originally gilded, made in Germany or Scandinavia. The design shows a bearded male head flanked by animal legs ending in paws. However, this head may also be meant to represent the god Woden. In this case, the objects beside his head would be understood as stylised ravens. In Anglo-Saxon mythology, Woden had two ravens which he sent out into the world to spy for him. When they returned, they sat on his shoulders and whispered their news into his ears. *K711, l: 48.8 mm*

Gold mount in the shape of a fish, decorated with filigree. It probably represents a pike, a fish well-known as an aggressive predator. *K1663, l: 300 mm*

Gold pommel cap, with cloisonné garnet decoration showing two animals seated face-to-face. Their necks are elongated and their heads turned back over their shoulders. Intertwined around their necks is what appears to be a two-headed serpent. The interlacing is an Anglo-Saxon feature, but the animals and the way they are seated may derive from the lions that appear on textiles and other luxury goods imported from the Mediterranean. *K284, l: 44 mm*

MEDITERRANEAN INFLUENCES

Although the Anglo-Saxons were originally pagans, Christian missionaries converted them during the seventh century. These missionaries introduced elements of Mediterranean culture, including completely new motifs and art styles. Newly-imported luxuries like illuminated manuscripts, textiles, carved ivories and painted panels exposed Anglo-Saxon craftspeople to these new influences, which would eventually have a major effect on their work.

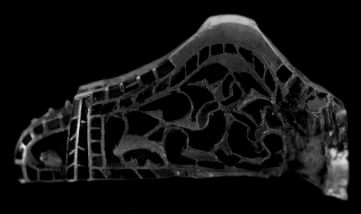

Stamped silver gilt foil fragment, with part of a line of warriors. *K1382, l: c.68 mm*

SWEDISH INFLUENCES

Some objects in the hoard show very strong Swedish connections, in particular hundreds of fragments of stamped silver foils which almost certainly once decorated a helmet. Many show warriors marching, kneeling or falling before their enemies. Very similar foils were used on the helmets found in rich warrior graves at Vendel and Valsgärde in central Sweden. The famous Sutton Hoo helmet is also decorated with foils like these.

CELTIC INFLUENCES

Seventh-century Britain was divided between the Anglo-Saxons in the east and the British Celts in the west. Many Mercians were of Celtic British descent, and Anglo-Saxon and British kings regularly fought both alongside and against each other, and often intermarried. Despite this, relatively little direct Celtic influence is visible in the Staffordshire Hoard.

In the later seventh century, a new art style began to emerge in Britain. Known as the 'Insular Style' and characterised by interlaced decoration, it combined elements from both the Germanic and Celtic traditions. Some of the later pieces in the hoard have animal decoration that is very close to that seen in early Insular Style illuminated manuscripts.

METHODS OF DECORATION

CLOISONNÉ

This technique involves creating a pattern of small cells (*cloisons*) that are then filled with cut stones or other material. Cloisonné garnet decoration had been popular in the later years of the Roman Empire and spread from there to the Germans and other peoples who lived beyond the Roman frontiers.

On the objects in the hoard, thin strips of gold were soldered to the base plate to create the cells. These cells were then partly filled with a paste that supported the other contents. Analysis of some of the pastes has shown that they were made of a beeswax-based material.

On top of the paste, the Anglo-Saxon metalworkers placed a small piece of gold foil – about the same thickness as modern kitchen foil – stamped with a die to produce a characteristic 'waffle' pattern. The lines making up this pattern are just one-fifth of a millimetre apart, demonstrating the incredible skill of the die engravers. The foil acted like a bicycle reflector: light passed through the garnet, hit the foil and

was reflected back through the garnet, making the object sparkle.

A piece of cut garnet was put in each cell on top of the gold foil. These garnets had been ground down until they were just over a millimetre thick and then cut to the shape needed for the pattern, possibly using a cutting wheel. The smallest pieces of garnet in the hoard are just a few millimetres long.

Finally, the metalworker rubbed over the surface of the cloisonné. Gold is quite a soft metal, so this process flattened and slightly spread out the tops of the cell walls, holding the garnets in place.

TOP ROW
Loose garnets which have fallen out of cloisonné-decorated objects in the hoard. *K1398*, LEFT TO RIGHT
l: 4.34 mm; l: 2.34 mm; l: 3.65 mm; l: 1.25 mm; l: 5.72 mm

BOTTOM ROW
Loose pieces of stamped gold foil that were originally set behind garnets. *K1399*, LEFT TO RIGHT
l: about 5 mm; l: c.3 mm; l: 2-3 mm

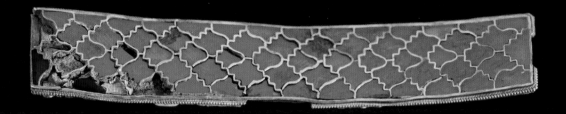

Decorative gold strip, with cloisonné garnet decoration. This strip is largely intact, but a few cells at one end have lost their garnets and reveal the gold foil or the paste below. *K273, l: 120 mm*

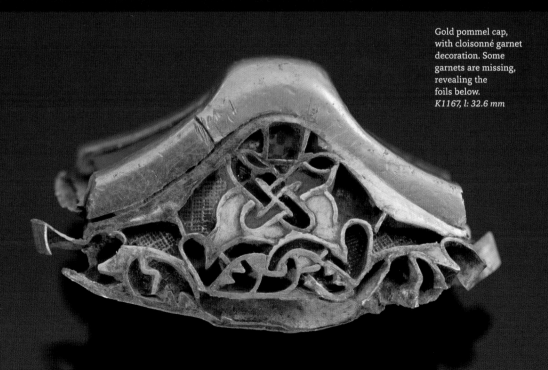

Gold pommel cap, with cloisonné garnet decoration. Some garnets are missing, revealing the foils below. *K1167, l: 32.6 mm*

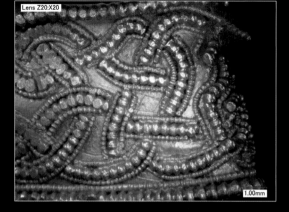

Lens Z20:X20

1.00mm

L=3.99 mm
L=0.36 mm
L=0.81 mm

TOP
Detail of the filigree
decoration on a gold
hilt collar (K308), at
x20 magnification.
Laying-out lines are
clearly visible at the
centre and towards
the bottom.

BOTTOM
Conservation
photomicrograph
showing the
measurements of
the wires and marks
on a filigree object.

FILIGREE

Filigree is made by soldering
metal wires to a metal base plate
to make patterns. In the hoard,
the filigree work is all in gold. We
think that the planned design was
usually scratched on to the base
plate before the wires were put in
place, and hid the scratched lines
from view. We can still see these
lines on a few hoard items where
the metalworker placed the wires
slightly out of position.

Looking closely at the filigree
from the hoard, we can see that the
pattern is made up of many short
lengths of wire. Each piece of the
pattern normally consists of three
pieces of wire, a thicker one in the
middle with a thinner one to each
side. The thicker wire is usually
about three-quarters of a millimetre
thick, the thinner ones about one-
third of a millimetre. The wires
were beaded or twisted to create
different decorative effects.

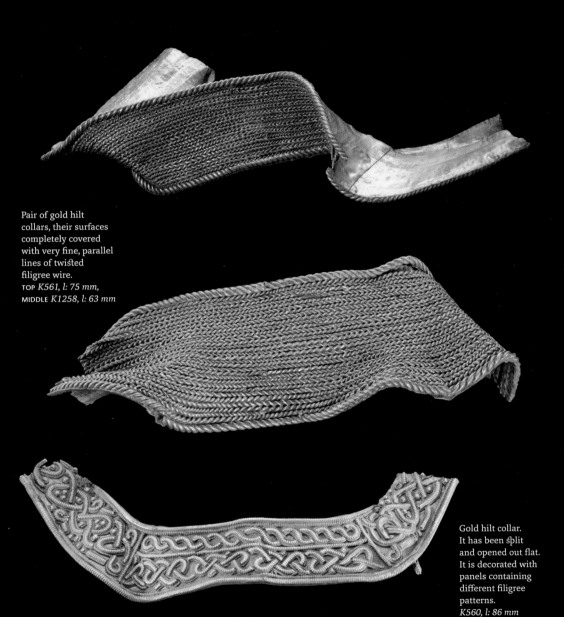

Pair of gold hilt
collars, their surfaces
completely covered
with very fine, parallel
lines of twisted
filigree wire.
TOP *K561, l: 75 mm,*
MIDDLE *K1258, l: 63 mm*

Gold hilt collar.
It has been split
and opened out flat.
It is decorated with
panels containing
different filigree
patterns.
K560, l: 86 mm

TOP
Fragments of stamped, silver-gilt foils with lines of warriors moving to the left and right.
K1423, for a total

BOTTOM
Fragments of stamped, silver-gilt foils showing a sequence of linked creatures with open jaws and back-turned heads.

STAMPING WITH DIES

The Staffordshire Hoard contains hundreds of fragments of thin silver foils with stamped decoration showing warriors and animals. The Anglo-Saxons used foils like these to decorate a variety of objects including bowls, drinking horns, scabbards and helmets. All the stamped foils found in the Staffordshire Hoard were made of silver and most of them were also gilded. A few original dies have been found elsewhere, all made of bronze.

Modern attempts to reproduce these foils have shown that they could have been made in a number of ways, but the following is one of the simplest. First the metalworker hammered out a piece of metal until he had a thin sheet. This sheet, less than half millimetre thick, was placed on top of the die. A piece of lead was placed on top of the metal sheet. The metalworker then hammered the lead, driving the sheet into the die and imprinting the design. The stamped sheet was then removed from the die and trimmed to size ready for use.

The finished foils were held in place by ribbed strips and small ribbed clips and fastened by little rivets and pins. The hoard contains many fragments of four different sizes of ribbed strip, a number of clips and dozens of loose pins.

Conservators at the British Museum have been piecing the foil fragments together to reveal the original patterns. It is difficult to be certain how the hoard foils were originally used, but Chris Fern, the Anglo-Saxon specialist who has been working on the Staffordshire Hoard research project, argues that some were almost certainly used to decorate a helmet.

Fragment of a stamped silver-gilt foil, which shows part of a line of facing male heads with prominent moustaches.
K1775, l: c.20 mm

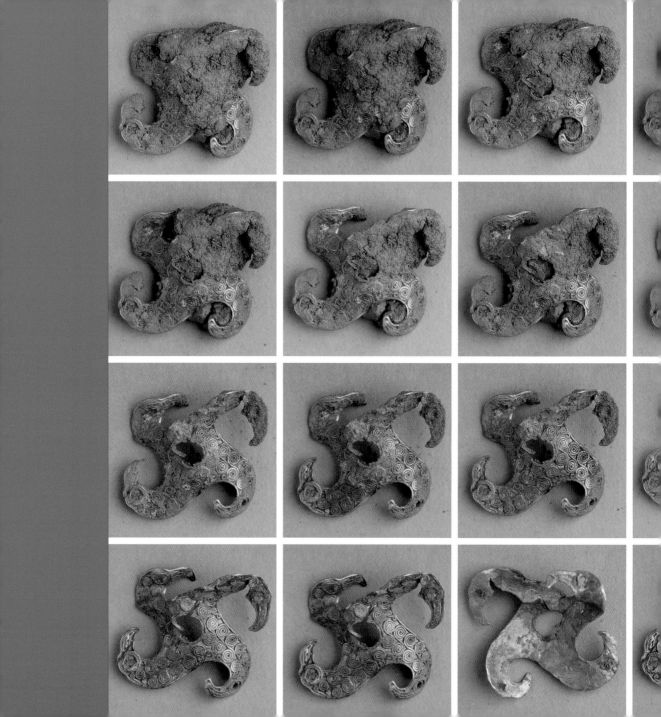

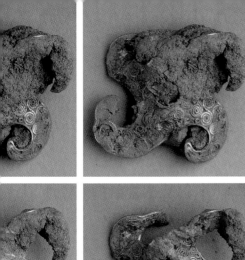
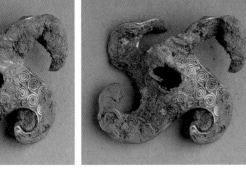
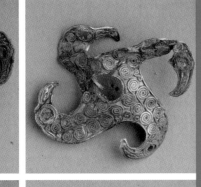

CONSERVATION
& RESEARCH

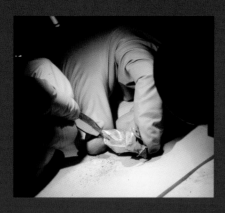

CONSERVATION PROCESS

When the Staffordshire Hoard objects arrived in the laboratory, the conservators were faced with a mass of objects, many still coated in soil. Each object was carefully recorded, photographed and assessed before it was cleaned. All the conservation work was done through a microscope and a full record was made at every stage.

Normally conservators use steel points to clean finds, but gold is soft and there was a risk that steel tools might mark the surfaces. The conservation team decided to try using thorns because they are sharp, flexible and softer than gold. They were a great success and all the hoard has been cleaned in this way. This technique means that the tool marks left on the objects by the Anglo-Saxon metalworkers are still clearly preserved.

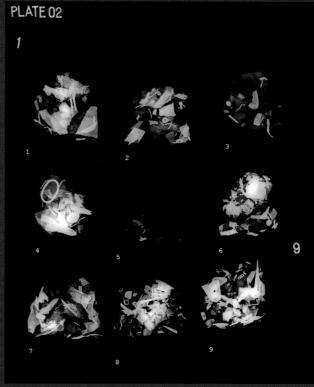

PLATE 02

1

1 2 3 4 5 6 7 8 9

Amongst the strangest objects that arrived in the conservation laboratory were about fifty small lumps of soil. X-rays showed that they contained small broken pieces of gold, fragments of silver foils, loose gold pins, cut garnets and gold foils. Some lumps contained several hundred individual fragments. The lumps were carefully taken apart by the conservators.

Using thorns to clean an object.

Xrays of some of the lumps of soil.

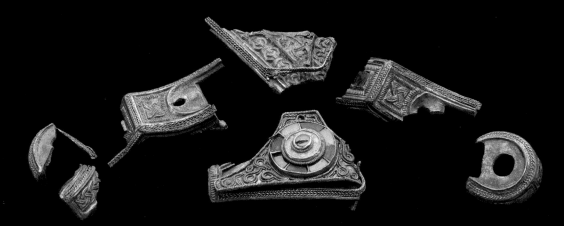

Fragments of a badly-broken silver pommel cap. One side was decorated with blue and white glass inlays.
Fragment with circular glass inlay K301, l: 32 mm

RIGHT
Gold hilt collar, badly damaged during removal from the sword handle.
K1118, l: 34 mm

Hoard piece showing damage before burying.
K667, l: 95 mm

Because the conservators would spend hours, or sometimes days, working on each item in the hoard, they became very familiar with them. As a result, they would often spot evidence that revealed more about the history of individual pieces. For example, they were often able to recognise pieces that belonged to the same object and reunite them.

People often assume that the hoard objects were damaged by ploughing while they were in the ground. However, very few pieces were damaged in this way. Most of the damage was caused when the pieces were stripped off the objects they were originally attached to.

The conservators and researchers also discovered clear signs of wear caused by frequent use on some items.

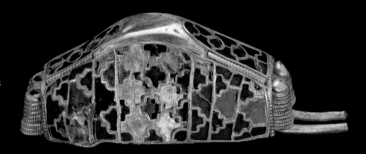

Gold pommel cap, from the top of a sword handle. The top of this pommel cap is very worn. It looks as if the owner often rested his hand on top of his sword handle when the sword was in its scabbard. Many pommel caps in the hoard have this kind of wear.
K353, l: 47.8 mm

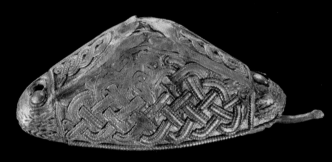

Gold pommel cap with cloisonné decoration. Two cells on one side are filled with pieces of red glass instead of garnets. The original garnets probably fell out and the person carrying out the repair either did not have access to new garnets or did not have the skill to cut them to shape. The pieces of glass are now weathered and dull, so they can easily be distinguished from the garnets, but originally they would have appeared identical.
K674, l: 45 mm

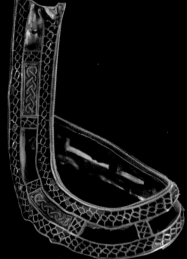

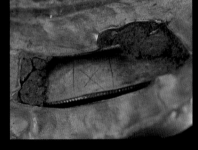

Gold slotted strip with manufacturing marks scratched on the back.
K513, l: 107 mm

Close examination during conservation also occasionally revealed what seem to be marks made by the Anglo-Saxon metalworkers to help them assemble the parts of an object correctly.

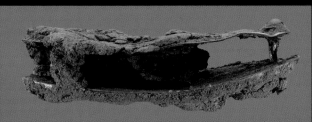

SCIENTIFIC ANALYSIS

The conservators and researchers are also investigating the materials used in the manufacture of the hoard, working with partner institutions in this country and abroad.

NIELLO

Niello is a black material made from a mixture of metallic sulphides used to decorate gold and silver objects or to highlight important details. Samples of niello from the hoard have been analysed at the British Museum and all the samples tested so far are a silver sulphide composition.

TOP
Silver mount, partly gilded and decorated with niello. Broken into more than a dozen pieces, this mount may be meant to represent a fish.
K82, l: c.165 mm

BOTTOM
Pair of gold hilt plates, still fastened together with the original gold nails. Traces of horn were found between the plates.
K283, l: 65 mm

ANALYSIS OF GOLD

Some of the gold objects from the Staffordshire Hoard have been analysed to discover their precise composition. Pure gold is very soft and needs to be alloyed, or mixed with other metals, to make it harder. The research is helping us to understand how the Anglo-Saxon metalworkers used different gold alloys for different purposes.

ORGANIC MATERIALS
(WOOD, HORN, BONE, ANTLER, TEXTILES, LEATHER)

While conserving some sword hilt plates, the conservators identified probable organic remains associated with them. Analysis at the British Museum suggested this was horn, probably from plates of horn that had originally been sandwiched between pairs of hilt plates. Another hilt plate produced traces of wood, which suggests that the original sword had a turned wooden handgrip.

THE STAFFORDSHIRE HOARD TRAIL PARTNERSHIP

The Staffordshire Hoard Trail Partnership brings together Birmingham Museums Trust, The Potteries Museum & Art Gallery, Lichfield Cathedral, Lichfield District Council, Tamworth Borough Council and Staffordshire County Council. The partnership tells the emerging story of the Staffordshire Hoard and the Anglo-Saxon history of the region, through a series of informative permanent and temporary displays and a programme of outreach activities aimed at residents and visitors alike.

VISIT THE OTHER SITES ON THE TRAIL TO FIND OUT MORE ABOUT THE HOARD AND ITS SETTING:

The Potteries Museum and Art Gallery, Stoke-on-Trent
The kingdom of Mercia and its place in the history of England.

Lichfield Cathedral
St Chad and the Christian background to the hoard, the St Chad Gospels and the Lichfield Angel.

Tamworth Castle
Anglo-Saxon warfare and kingship.

ACKNOWLEDGEMENTS

The Staffordshire Hoard is owned by Birmingham City Council and Stoke-on-Trent City Council on behalf of the nation, and cared for by Birmingham Museums Trust and the Potteries Museum & Art Gallery, Stoke-on-Trent.

The Staffordshire Hoard was reported as a find under the Treasure Act 1996, which requires all similar finds to be declared. The Portable Antiquities Scheme officers are the first point of contact for all archaeological finds made by members of the public.

The Staffordshire Hoard was acquired with donations from members of the public following a huge campaign led by the Art Fund, the national fundraising charity for art. The acquisition was also generously supported by the National Heritage Memorial Fund, Birmingham City Council, Stoke-on-Trent City Council, Wartski, and many other trusts and foundations, and corporate philanthropy.

The Staffordshire Hoard Gallery was supported by the Heritage Lottery Fund, Garfield Weston, The City of Birmingham Museums & Art Gallery Development Trust, The Friends of Birmingham Museums Trust, Arts Council England, and The J Paul Getty Jnr Charitable Trust.

The major research project now being conducted on the Staffordshire Hoard is supported by Historic England, and a number of other trusts and foundations. We would like to thank the many individuals and organisations who are valued partners in the research project. The learning and outreach programmes are supported by a number of trusts and foundations.

We are very grateful to the thousands of members of the public who donated towards the acquisition of the Staffordshire Hoard and who continue to support the conservation and research.

We would like to thank History West Midlands for their support and commitment to telling the story of the Staffordshire Hoard.

For full details of our partners and funders
www.staffordshirehoard.org.uk/partners

www.staffordshirehoard.org.uk